TWENTY POEMS

Kathrin Schmidt
TWENTY POEMS

Selected, translated
& introduced by
Sue Vickerman

PUBLICATIONS
2020

Published by Arc Publications,
Nanholme Mill, Shaw Wood Road
Todmorden OL14 6DA, UK
www.arcpublications.co.uk

978 1910345 44 3

Design by Tony Ward
Printed by ImprintDigital.com, Upton Pyne, Exeter, Devon

Cover image:
Detail of porcelain scultpure by Nuala O'Donovan
Photograph by Tony Ward

ACKNOWLEDGEMENTS

Kathrin Schmidt's poems in the original German are taken
from the following publications and are reproduced by kind
permission of the poet: *Poesiealbum 179*, (Verlag Neues Leben,
Berlin 1982); *Ein Engel fliegt durch die Tapetenfabrik*, (Verlag Neues
Leben, Berlin, GDR 1987); *go-in der belladonnen*, (Kiepenheuer
& Witsch, Köln 2000); *Blinde Bienen, Gedichte*, (Kiepenheuer &
Witsch Verlag 2010; *waschplatz der kühlen dinge*, (Kiepenheuer
und Witsch, Köln, 2018)
    Some of these poems in translation have appeared in *The
Poetry Review, The Stockholm Review,* and *nomansland*. 'Patterned
with rutsches' served as subtitles for Betina Kuntzsch's film-short
Schneestaub (2019).
    The translator, Sue Vickerman, is grateful to Arts Council
England for a 2018 award to translate Kathrin Schmidt's poems
and respond with her own, and a 2019 award to develop the
project further under the mentorship of Fiona Sampson.

Supported using public funding by
ARTS COUNCIL
ENGLAND

Arc Chapbook Series
Series Editor: Tony Ward

Contents

Introduction: a Passion Project / 6

Introduction: a Passion Project

The trigger for this work of translation was the UK's 2016 decision to leave Europe. I joined the national soul-searching. Some German friends commiserated, themselves soul-searching over the rise of the far-right *Alternativ für Deutschland* (AfD) in the regions of the former German Democratic Republic.[1] I found myself dwelling on parallels I'd noticed, years before, between my own childhood and those of friends who'd grown up in the GDR:[2] left-behind feelings; cultural loss (*too many immigrants*); disadvantage; *things were better when...* Were there not similarities in my parents' and other Brexit-voters' views of the way things have gone, and the views of today's east German AfD-voters?

Wanting to understand, I picked a poet from the "left-behind east" to translate, also wanting, somehow, to compensate for our newly ruptured relationship with Europe through translating poetry,[3] because I'm a poet. I searched for a kindred spirit roughly my age, politically left, a woman. Skimming Kathrin Schmidt's poems I could see some were feminist, and addressed political issues. And I liked the fact that in 1989 she was part of the round-table discussions on the future of the two Germanys as a representative of the reunification-sceptic United Left, meetings she later described as *a dreadful men's club*, and which fuelled her feminist fire. Post-reunification she did a stint editing the East Berlin-founded women's magazine *Ypsilon*. Also attractive was Kathrin's literary success: winner of the German Book Prize (2009) for her novel *Du Stirbst Nicht*[4]

---

[1] There are AfD voters Germany-wide but their concentration in former GDR regions is said to be due to *Osis* feeling "left behind" since Germany's 1990 reunification (by some measures, a well-founded grievance).
[2] I discovered these affinities when living in east Berlin in the early 'nineties. West German friends had grown up in relative affluence.
[3] I am now contracted to translate Kathrin's short story collection *It's over. Don't go there.*
[4] *You're not dying*, translation by Christina Les, Naked Eye Publishing 2021

and winner of the prestigious Leonce-und-Lena poetry award. How come Kathrin Schmidt was still completely unknown in the Anglophone world? Apart from a mere six poems,[5] I found none of Kathrin's (then) five poetry collections, five novels or thirty-one short stories in English.[6] This clinched my decision.

These twenty poems draw together work from five of Kathrin's six collections published before and after Reunification (1990). While some poems in her œuvre use forms, the ones I've chosen to translate are all in her more habitual free metrics which allow greater scope for her audacious, experimental syllabic twists and turns.

Kathrin's irrepressible poetic style eludes classification. She uses words intensively, employing every conceivable technique and device: clever puns; tongue-twisting alliteration and assonance; the playful moving of consonants, Jandl-style, to release unexpected meanings – such difficult inventions,[7] such labyrinthine nuances, word after word attention-demanding to the point of exhaustion! Translating Kathrin had my brain doing double-flips.[8]

I couldn't *not* translate the title poem of Kathrin's perhaps most acclaimed collection (2000), *go-in der belladonnen,*[9] 'day of the drop-dead divas'. In this "ode to Berlin" the dominating ("masculine") west and disadvantaged ("female") east are in a face-off.[10] It's a cynical take on Germany's reunification that

---

[5] Translated by Australian poet Gig Ryan, see *lyrikline.org.*
[6] Jamie Osborne has since had several translations of Kathrin's poems published (*TLS, nomansland, Blackbox Manifold*), most from her collection *Blinde Bienen,* (KiWi Verlag, 2010).
[7] I would email Kathrin for an explanation, then make up an English word that would do a similar job.
[8] Kathrin told me that once, as an invited participant in an international poet-to-poet translation event (German to Arabic), she alone was left un-translated by the end: not one of the translators would take on the challenges of her poetic language.
[9] It took me three years to settle on a translation of the title alone, having discussed it with practically every German-speaker of my acquaintance.
[10] East German women bore the brunt of reunification, says Kathrin, and this poem is about their disadvantaged new circumstances.

touches on nearly all Kathrin's themes as a writer: gender; identity; the body; eroticism; her own lived history; language itself. This poem demonstrates her baroque style *par excellence*.[11] Its words *have bubbles round them which partially overlap each other in meaning, forming new intersecting layers,* as Kathrin put it, with one word serving to throw up a whole new idea and lurch the reader breathlessly into the next mini-scene – an explosive, relentless zooming-on. Like T. S. Eliot's *The Wasteland*, it has an epic feel, densely packed with references and allusions that often require "insider" knowledge of places and circumstances which Kathrin herself says are possibly only recognisable by her own GDR peers. Like *The Wasteland*, it could do with its own Brodie's Notes all by itself, which would probably be even longer than this chapbook (I have not, for now, annotated it, or any other poems).

Challenge upon challenge. In the first line of 'birdknacks' (*vogelallüren*), the word *weltgemacht* plays on *wettgemacht* (compensatory, redressing, extenuating, or making up for something). The playfully changed consonant invents a word that has further meaning layered on. I thought to retain something of the sense of "redressing", hence my decision to use "world-counteracting", which, furthermore, works rhythmically in the line. In the final line is another invented word, *flügeltiere*, on the face of it, "winged creatures"; native Germans will, however, spot the fun association with *Flügeltüre*, the name of a crazy "gull-winged" novelty of a car from the 1970s, the doors of which opened by rising upwards, giving the striking appearance of birds' wings. This association with a wacky supersonic invention is a witty harking-back to the poem's opening declaration, that birds are highly technologically gifted because they are able to fly, while refugees are left (suffering) on land.

Every translator's personal agenda impacts on what and how they translate. The political dissent I believed I spotted in

---

[11] Kathrin's supreme understatement: *it's a poem that plays with language a lot.*

the poem 'paperworks' (how risky! And not even censored? I thought) made me select it. Published in 1987 in the GDR, the poem demonstrated (as I saw it) how wordplay and punning had been useful devices for sidelong criticism of the régime. The paperworks' guardian angel dutifully criticises Western culture's *cola und kitsch*, while mocking the factory management's pretended benevolence, the canteen's "delicious" soup which in truth has no goodness in it.

I've felt better about having come to this project as an "outsider translator" since participating in a Zoom discussion[12] with poet and poetry translator Iain Galbraith. The act of translation, says Iain, begins with looking and listening. He described his pastime of solitary fishing in his young teens as having been formative to his eventual translation process. In those years of fishing, he learned to interpret into language images of water and trees, and sounds of silence. According to Iain (and others before him)[13] we "read", then translate to ourselves, all that we see and hear.

Well, I never got into fishing. But I did learn in my early years to "read" a Bradford housing estate, at first glance grey and homogenous, with its street sounds of milk-float, hopscotch and rag-and-bone man, followed, from the age of nine, by the whole new world of a peaceful, cherry tree lined cul-de-sac in Oxfordshire. And some of this, and of everything since, has been translated into my creative writings.

Everybody is a translator.

Sue Vickerman

[12] Iain Galbraith was the special guest at the *Stammtisch* discussion run by Rebecca DeWald, Glasgow Goethe Institut, August 2020

[13] Jacques Derrida and other post-structuralists have suggested that writing is itself a form of translation because it is an act of interpretation and of positing meaning. i.e. a so-called "original" text is itself already a translation, as "derivative and heterogenous" as the translated text. See Derrida J., 'Des Tours de Babel', in *Difference in Translation*, Cornell University Press, Ithaca & New York, 1985.

*"Who we choose to translate is political.
How we choose to translate
is political."*

JEN HOFER, JOHN PLUECKER
Manifesto for Ultratranslation, 2013

PUBLISHERS' NOTE

Use of punctuation and capitals was intermittent among Schmidt's poems until at least 1987. All poems dated from 2000 onward in the original German are without capital letters for headings, nouns and at the start of sentences and are devoid of almost all punctuation, the latter device being a German poetic convention adopted by some contemporary poets, sometimes explained as an endeavour to "equalize" words. The translator accordingly omits capitals and punctuation in her translation.

handwerk

ich halte mich schräg
auf den graten
der täglichen sprache
vielfruchtbaum,
braucht sie den schlag aller wetter
mitten ins mark
die sprache
dies menschlichste fleisch
(und oft in konserven
aus rostigem schrott)
sie liegt auf dem nagelbrett
das wir ihr hinstelln
mit abendaltem gewäsch
und blanken bilanzen

die scheibe dreht sich:
töpfer formen die worte
schüssel und krug
zerbrechlich
und immer ein raum

wordsmithing

im stood off kilter
on the burred bark
of everyday speechs
bounteous tree,
need it weather all these assaults
on root and branch
this speech thats
the raw meat of us –
a product often left
in rusting cans to rot
it lies on the bed of nails
we set down for it
beneath stale worn sheets of words
and bland blanket statements

the wheel is turning:
ceramicists mould wordshapes
dish and flagon
form new and
delicate speechscapes

'ich leb nie aus...'

ich leb nie aus
was aus den jahren fiel
an bitterbittrem
und an augenschön

als schlüg ich
nägel
in das helle wasser ein
das tagwärts fließt
und hielt mich daran
fest

vorm bäcker

mit krähenfedern
blaut der rauch
den himmel
und die versuchung
bäckt in jenem ofen:
brot zu essen
aus hunger und lust
zugleich

'im still snagged on...'

im still snagged on
the hitches of those years
the bitterest bits
the beautifulest

nails ive knocked
so to speak
into the bright new waters
racing dawnwards
on which im stuck
hooked

outside the bakery

smokes ravening plumes
billow blue
heavenwards
and temptation
is baking in that oven:
the taking of bread
whereby hunger and lust
are one

dank

ich trage stets zu dünne jacken,
um die wetterbesser mitzukriegen.
aber das ist nur möglich wegen
des honigs, den du schon
in heißer milch gelöst hast,
wenn ich komme.

du schliefst schon

ich bügelte noch,
während ich eigentlich
eilig dir zutrieb, spät war es,
müde mein arm,
und die spitze des eisens
brach ein riss
in die haut deiner haut, dein hemd
o wie du stöhntest, verletzt,
aus dem schwarz

thanks to

i have a thing for flimsy jackets
as a way of savouring the weather.
this is only made practicable
by honey, already
stirred into hot milk by you,
when i get home.

you were asleep already

i was still ironing,
although in fact I was
rushing to join you, it was late,
my arm hurting,
and the tip of the iron
nicked into
the fabric of your skin, your shirt
o how you whimpered, injured,
out of the dark

Korrosion

Der Ton sollte das Schweigen der Frau ausweiden
wie ein Geschlachtetes. Er wollte es dann, wie man
den Truthahn stopft, füllen mit Augenblick, Bier und
                                                Belohnung.
Sie indes sass, die rosigen Schenkel verschert, über dem
lautlosen Schinken, biss zwischendurch die kleinen
                                                Gelenke
der Finger und schwieg, 'Der Ton!' Schwieg sie. 'Davon kann
ich nicht leben'. Und starb nicht, obwohl sie
vom Schinken gewürgt wurde. So, auf den Scherben seiner
Beherrschung, verdarb sie sich. Magen, Füsse und Haaransatz
waren längst ungeniessbar, als er den Ton zurück in den
                                                Mund
nahm. Sie aber weinte, worunter der Tag unhörbar zu
                                                rosten begann
und in der Mitte zerbrach.

picasso

der eine linie auszieht, die in wirklichkeit
eine frau ist. der eine nackte, ausgezogene
frau in ein bild zieht, das in meinem ausweis
falsch wäre, obwohl es mich bildet

Corrosion

The tune was supposed to scour out his wife's mute state
like picking a carcass clean. Then, like stuffing a turkey
he intended to fill her up with leers, beer and bonuses.
But she squatted atop the dumb ham, her rose-pink thighs
                                                    scissored,
gnawing her finger's dainty knuckles, still keeping mum.
                                        The tune –
she thought, staying dumb – doesn't do it for me.
And she didn't succumb, despite the fact
of being strangled by the ham. What she did get off on
was his total loss of control. When at last he took the tune
back in his mouth, the allure of belly, feet and cowlick had
                                                    passed.
But she wept at that, whereupon without a sound the day
                                        began to rust
and reaching the middle, snapped.

picasso

who man-oeuvres a line, which man-ifests as a
woman. a clothing-removed nude, man-oeuvred
to depict woman, which as my ID would be
disallowed, although it depicts me.

'So simpel hängt der Winter herab...'

So simpel hängt der Winter herab
wie eine Windel. Komm,
fahrn wir schatten halbieren,
schneiden wir Mittagswunden dem
frostigen Tag! Alles ist unverletzt.
aus den Offsetdrucken lächeln
die tüchtigen Alten, ein junger Athlet
verschwindet im meinem Kaffee
nach der Schraube. Ich gebe ihm fünf Punkte,
da hat er doch nichts verloren.
So simpel klingelt das Gold.
Komm,
lass uns fingerspitz reden!
Du sprichts nicht. Du krümelst.
Du ziehst ein Messer
durch die Butter.
Du hebst einen Stein auf
meine Brüste.
Du brichst meine druckschwarze Mundkruste nicht,
du lässt mich nicht bluten.
So simpel sind wir verschneit.

'Winter is hanging so pure out there...'

Winter is hanging so pure out there
like a nappy. Come on,
let's go carve our shadows in it,
cut it up for lunch
this frosty day! It's so intact.
From the junk-mail pile pensioners
smile, worldly-wise. A young athlete
drops right into my coffee-cup
after a corkscrew dive. I give him five points
not a penalty.
His medal clinks, so pure.
Hey
let's get down to the nitty-gritty!
You don't speak. You make crumbs.
You slither a knife
through the butter.
You pick a seed
off my breast.
You don't penetrate my ink-daubed crumby mouth.
You don't make me bleed.
So pure are we, snowed in.

tapetenfabrik

ein engel fliegt durch die tapetenfabrik.
ein baumwollner krieg ist sein hemd
gegen glasfaser, cola und kitsch.
freundlich wird gegrüsst, wenn er sie überschwebt,
die arbeiter, auf seiner göttlichen posaune reitet
und täglich die fenster putzt,
was keiner sonst tut.
er sieht aus wie engelbrechts längst verstorbene frau,
die ihn noch täglich zur arbeit schickt.
in der pause isst man aspik, aus dem fisch glotzt.
den ersten haps bekommt der fabrikengel,
der inzwischen ganz sicher seine posaune geputzt hat
und musiziert, zur verschönerung der geräusche.
so bläst er zum kampf um lustgewinn
bei der herstellung von billigtapeten.
so bleiben die leute fröhlich,
als er die nachrichten der bbc verkündet
und die entsprechende offerte von tass.
die tassen scheppern, wenn er am mittag
eine himmlische brühe austeilt und an die toten schweine
erinnert, falls es eisbein gibt.
der fabrikengel ist eine laus
im pelz der planung, die unbekannte variable.
tapetenmeter ergeben weltumspannende rollen.
das weiss der fabrikengel, wenn er zum schichtschluss
einnickt und runterfällt.

paperworks

an angel is flapping through the paperworks.
his frock is flannelette in protest at
synthetic fibres, plastic tat and pepsi.
greetings float up as he circles
the workers astride his holy horn,
giving the windows a daily clean
that otherwise wouldnt get done.
he has a look of gabriels wife; long-dead
she still packs him off on his daily shift.
break is tinned fish snacks, goggle-eyes in aspic.
first dibs goes to the works angel
whos playing his highly-sheened horn
to ameliorate the din.
his campaign is for ever-increasing pleasure
in the production of cheap wallpaper.
he makes the masses happy
by passing on news from the bbc
alongside the tass bulletins.
at noon pots rattle when, dishing out
an ambrosial slop, he prays for dead pigs
in case theres a trace of pork content.
the works angel has got under the skin
of the planning department, a loose cannon.
wallpapers are marching on, making their mark.
they've got clout. the works angel learns this when,
at shift's end, no longer alert, he plummets.

wie du die tür schließt

und gehst: bis eben
ein stets wiederholbarer vorgang.
kämst du jetzt wieder,
deine stimme spräch inselchen
auf den kahlschlag in meinem kopf

eben noch stumm

in ihren schwappenden fruchtwasserblasen,
kommen die kleinen marktführer endlich
zu stimme: im stottern, das über die zunge
poltert, im bocksschrei dem findelvater entglitten,
der leermutter die nullstelle gerutscht.
einige werden das faltgeflügel der laken
bewundern, wie es den ton hält
im schrank, andere werden der folgezeit
schillernde zukunft entlocken. in der es
ans marktführen geht. in der über den strassen
wieder betrunken die schürzen flattern, nüchterne
jäger vorm bauch, eben noch stumm.

how you close the door

and leave: until now
an invariable everyday act.
if you now came back
your voice would be a small island
on my heads clear-felled wasteland

still keeping mum

in a sloshing whoosh of afterbirth lather,
baby market-leaders at last have their say
in stutters that erupt from the tongue,
a billy-goat's bellow escaping the foster-father,
rent-a-womb mum clocking back to zero.
some will love the bed-linen – its wingtucked folds
dovetailing, how it keeps up the tone
in the cupboard, while others relish the bling glimmer
of the coming era. of market leadership.
in which, above the streets, the pinnies will flap,
tipsy again; in which hardened hunters will go on
hunting for bellies, still keeping mum.

go-in der belladonnen

im oberwasser berlins ein rumoren: breitblättrig,
außer fasson, schlägt die zunge ein rad. wer heut eine ubahn
                            beherrscht,
hat morgen gut lachen. wer heut eine bank überstimmt, ist
                                morgen
nicht nackt. die stimme des filters säuselt aus den gebäuden:
o laß dich durchsaugen vor dem gang in den fettnapf,
den handlangerstatus. belladonnen am hammerklavier
in der philharmonie, belladonnen im pub und im kaufrausch,
                             belladonnen
in den bettelschächten der züge, belladonnen im laken. wenn
                          eine nicht bellt,
wird sie gleich für den hund gehalten, der immerfort schweigt,
und mitleids gefüttert. so wird sie dann wirklich nie zu den
bellen, den donnen gehören. der sturz aus der klaviatur
scheint ein ratschluß von innen, ein silberblick des geschlechts.
überdauert ein tier, heißt das frühling in unbestrittener
                              sprache.
die frau hat der frühlinge ein oder zwei, je nach haut
und behaarung. gib atropin in die lidfalte, und du wirst
                        dein grünblaues
wunder erleben dürfen: den zuspruch der stadt, des
                        kreuzorträtsels,
das sich nicht lösen läßt. noch die sektoren
versuchen den männlichen akt miteinander.
am oberbaumbrückengeländer klebt, wenn ich zeiten
                        wechsle zu fuß,
eine trockene fliege – ich weiß leider nicht, wie insekten
als mumien aussehen müssen, ich denk es mir nur und
                        kratze sie ab
in den dreck, der wenigstens ehrlich am boden liegt: arme alte
und haut, die sich schuppt und erneuert, als wärs der
                        amphibie
darunter nun doch nicht egal in ihrem wechselhellen getue.

the day of the drop-dead divas

in berlin's emboldened backwaters, rumblings: half-blathered,
the tongues of the pot-bellied turning cartwheels. today's
                              metro masters
are laughing all the way to the bank. today's bank execs are
                              laughing so hard
they're wetting themselves. the air-cons purr from the office blocks:
just get in quick, don't miss a trick, before you're sucked
                              down the piss-pan
and wash up washing dishes. drop-dead divas on posh pianos
at the philharmonic, drop-dead divas in wine-bars, on shopping
                              sprees, drop-dead divas
under the arches, drop-dead divas between the sheets. she who
                              doesn't act the diva
will be deemed the type of bitch who quietly submits and
lets herself be kept – the likes of whom will never be esteemed
as one of them, a drop-dead, a diva. the piano crescendos –
its inner summons a woman's come-on look shot sidelong.
putting it simply, the fittest survive to see another spring.
a woman who follows a skin care regime and depilates
                              will win
her second spring. drop deadly nightshade in your eyes and
                              they'll widen
to a nasty surprise: riotous cheers for the metropolis
whose crossroad-puzzle is yet to be resolved. the allied sectors
intent as ever on mutual buggery.
stuck to the oberbaum bridge, when i swap zones on foot, is a
                              dried-out fly's
corpse. sadly i haven't the faintest clue what insects must look like
as mummies, i think to myself, and scrape her up from the filth
                              that lies – at least
in the open – all around, poor old lass; and this skin that sloughs
                              off and
regenerates itself as if the amphibienne within gives more than
                              a damn
after all – her with her fickle, lightning-quick posture-shifts.

aus ihren augen beschießen die belladonnen den fluß,
der die spree sich zu nennen niemals bereit war, wie er dir
glaubwürdig mitteilt, wenn du ihn fragst. am besten lüpfst
                                            du dazu den
breitbekrempelten hut und schöpfst dir den schluck,
der auskunft gibt, direkt in den hals. nicht amaryllen
säumen den weg in die wohnungen, aus denen batisten
                                            gesänge
von hausfrauen herwehn. männer wie pottwale stoßen amber
aus ihrem gedärm in die versiegelte luft. belege ich bald
einen atemkurs, soll mir statt besserung blühen: der
                              schließmuskelkrampf.
im aufgeschnittenen blick trägt die fröschin heut grausame
                                            wünsche.
die alkaloide sind weiblich geworden in diesem jahrhundert
und jagen uns durch den schlaf in die schönheit.
belladonnen am hammerklavier in den mittleren schichten,
                                            belladonnen
in kneipe und supermarkt, belladonnen mit handlangerstatus.
                              der fettnapf
mit amber gefüllt, auf daß noch die letzte männliche lust
                              ihren ofen verläßt.
pottwal im schlickwasser spree, schlachtschiff im darmdunst
des stadtvolkes: das kommt heraus, wenn bellen und
                              donnen von oben herab
berlin einfach aufsagen wollen als ein gedicht. verhaltenen
                                            schritts
geht ein münzrundes weib in friedrichshagen unter dem
                              wasser hindurch.
das ist immer noch mehr, als jesus von nazareth dunnemals
oben probierte, denk ich. und mache
den knick in den knicks, die beuge ins beugen. und lächle.
und lasse mich kommen aus all meinen schießscharten.

the divas are shooting drop-dead looks, bombarding the river
who will proclaim, if you ask him, he isn't to blame for
taking the name
spree. best thing is, simply tip your city gent's bowler
and swallow his protestation down in one. like a shot.
not a single bourgeois amaryllis adorns the boulevard
to the apartment blocks whence the songs of housewives
waft, tissue-thin.
pot-bellied whale-men shit precious excrement out of their
innards
into the suffocating air. i'm off to attend a breathing class,
not exactly to de-stress, just make my own tight-spasmed
sphincter relax.
to cut to the quick: today's frog-esses are harbouring
fiendish desires.
in this very century alkaloid compounds have turned
feminine
and pound through us during our beauty-sleep. drop-dead divas
on posh pianos for the aspirational, drop-dead divas down
the local,
in the superstore. drop-dead divas washing dishes. piss-pan
packed with precious shit, enough to make the half-dead
dog out back slope in
for one last sniff. the sperm whale stuck in the spree's filthy
muck – battleship
in the gut of the citizenry – peeks out when the drop-deads,
the divas up top
want to simply speak berlin like a poem. in friedrichshagen
a weighty wench, worth it in gold, walks with regal bearing
under the water. better in my view than jesus of nazareth's
shot at walking atop it. by miles. and I form
the most curt of curtseys, a barely bowing bow, and smile.
and with guns ablaze from all my slits, make myself come.

verspielt

und der bussard verlor die beeren,
die er unter den flügeln trug. er segelte
um die dorfkirche, deren schatten
sich über den anger spannte. ein mädchenkind
sprang quer übern platz, seine beinchen
sprachen im wechsel fraktur
von der vor ihm liegenden zeit, die zöpfe,
verflochten mit luftsträhnen, pfefferten
so schnelle takte auf seine schultern, dass unsere blicke
das geschmetter nicht einholen konnten. nur langsam
kamen wir der vorstellung näher, es könnte
unsere tochter sein.

muster, geloopt

im schnee hatten wir nichts zu verlieren, das uns beunruhigte.
aus allen wolken gefallen, sinterten die kristalle
zu straffem eistaft unter dem schmelzpunkt. ich weiß noch,
wie wir versuchten, ihn zu zerschneiden mit unseren kufen.

ein schneesample kroch uns ins ohr, wir loopten es,
dass es uns wieder und wieder hinaufzog und aufzog.
auch zeit rodelte neben uns her, das ende im blick.
was dort seinen anfang nahm, würden wir nicht mehr wissen.

das mochte ein vorteil sein, doch wir teilten ihn nicht.
versuchten, uns sichtbar zu halten im cloudstaub.
solange es sparsam graupelte, freuten wir uns
am glück, das an intakten fäden über uns hing –

während sie einzureißen begannen, wechselte seine bestimmung:
wir wurden gebrechlich und hielten nicht stand,
als es vom himmel fiel. in großen stücken verschwand es,
riss loops und samples aus auge und ohr.

swapped

and the buzzard let go the berries
he'd been carrying under his wings, and soared
around the village church whose shadow
was looming over the common. a little girl
skipped across the square, stick legs
tap-dancing the split-second
timing in which he would act, her plaits,
interspersed with snatched breaths, ratatating
rapid raps on his axillae, our eyes
not quick enough to take in the attack. at last
after several moments had passed we grasped the fact
it could be our daughter.

patterned with rutsches

in the snow we just let go. nothing to lose. no worries.
crystals falling out of the wide blue yonder vitrified:
taut flat ice satin. way below zero. thinking back –
what an effort we made! slicing it up with our sledge's runners.
a snowschlupf chilled us to the eyeballs. we rutsched it.
got pulled round and up, round, and up, again and again.
but time itself was sledging beside us, portending the end.
something was starting that wasnt ours to comprehend.

perhaps it was better that way. to be unaware.
holding out. our shapes holding out in the cyberhaze.

while the flake-fall was still light, we were happy with
the fate that hung above us on untampered-with threads
but, as these began to fray and split, our destiny took on a
different shape. we became unstable, unable to stand as it
fell and fell from the sky, dropped in huge chunks,
ripped rutsches and schlupfs from our orifices.

31

hier, in der warteschleife auf den entscheidenden cut,
schneidest du das verschwundene blau deiner jacke zurück
ins erinnern.
damit wieder enzian ist, wenn die kleinen gewitter unter meinen
gestrickten matronenhülsen noch einmal zu knistern beginnen.

amazonian amazon

auf meinem konto keine krümmung der jahrezeit,
kein wetterleuchten vom krisenblitz.
wie er einschlug, die faule kiste zum platzen zu bringen,
trug sich anderswo zu. nicht wert der rede,
die meinen mund ansonsten bewegt. das haus
hängt der bank zwar zum hals raus, damit sie ihn
nimmermehr vollkriegt, das geld aber, nett gebeutelt,
geht brav seinen flüssigen weg. kein griechenland
spiegelt sich drin, dem die schuld
übern kragen wächst. wenn der platzt,
hörst du im wüten washingtons *trumpet*, wie
übern atlantischen ozean ostwärts gespielt. welche einigkeit
zwischen den klängen verschiedener seiten. welches
trommelfell, das sich spannt, links zum trotz, rechts zum schur.
nach billigen indern für den nur halbwegs
sauberen haushalt steht mir kein sinn,
und dennoch klagt die amazone in mir
offene grenzen ein. spricht's
und legt die weibliche endung beiseite.
ich schaue dem e hinterher, meinem
blauen, so blauen begehr.

now, on continuous loop awaiting the final schnitt,
a flash-back: your jacket's faded blue gives rise to a memory.
it is gentian once more, and the little cap-guns beneath the
                                                    home-knitted
liberty-bodice encasing my bosom start popping again.

amazonisch amazon

no sign of a seasonal dip in my bank account,
no lightning after the thunderbolt.
though meant to bust open that rotten barrel, it passed over
and went elsewhere. say no more. i wont waste words
that can move my mouth for things worthwhile. my house
is ever in the banks stranglehold, never
will it let go. but my money, although hard done-to,
digs its honest furrow. fat chance greece will follow,
its debt grown way down below
its collar. if it crashes, youll hear
how the washington trumpet's herald of rage
blazes easterly over the atlantic. such harmony in the tunes
being played on all the various sides. how the drum
reverberates left for spite, right for incitement.
i hate the thought of importing cheap asians
to bottom this households badly mopped-up
mess, and yet the amazon woman in me
battles for open borders,
speaks out, setting the *her* of herself aside.
i look back at her as she passes, hung
in the air, my animus.

faulwasser

geläutert von der wasserfäule
steht das ried, als wolle es hoch hinaus
aus dem schlick. bein an bein
jagen wasserläufer dem spiegel
den glanz ab. brackige luft, mein lungenkraut
säuert den atem, schweißtreibend,
schleimlösend. gestilltes blut
unter den haut, hab ich den ausblick gern,
der den himmel auf seine flüssigen schultern nimmt.

leihfrist

monatenlang schlief ich rückwärts,
auf kindheit zu, während die tage dir
fremdwörter liehen. meine, deine.
komm, wir lassen uns gendern! aber
der abschied lief längst aus deinem
in meinen hals, bis er voll davon war
und ich endlich aufwachen konnte.
über mich hängt nun mein immer noch
schlafendes kleid, es soll von mir träumen:
wie ich es langsam zu füttern beginne mit mir.
wie es mich einverleibt und zu kichern beginnt
aus all seinen knopflöchern. wie es den reißverschluss
gar nicht mehr zu kriegen kann.
aber es baumelt nur leis, und ich seh dich von ferne
ins ungewiss schwimmen, mein eben
verschlüpfter fisch.

stagnant

laundered by the tank's foul flow
the reed stands tall as if to get ahead,
shun the slime. strut by strut
wading birds disrupt the glossy lustre
of its surface. brackish air, my lung linctus
causes bad breath, hot sweats,
loosened mucus. blood lurks
under the dermis. i love this landscape,
how it carries the sky on its waterlogged shoulders.

borrowing time

i slept for months in reverse mode,
sliding into childhood, meanwhile the times
were lending you borrowed words. mine. your.
lets get sexed! but the gender divide
that had stuck in your craw way back
was now stuck in mine, till finally i
swallowed it and got my consciousness.
hanging above me now, not conscious
yet, my frock. im what it gets off on.
watch how i start slowly feeding it with bits of me.
how it swallows my body, begins to snicker
out of every buttonhole. how it can no longer
manage to close its zipper.
it is swishing. softly. meanwhile i watch you from far off,
swimming into the blue, my newly
en-gendered fish.

natürlich gesprochen

die abende kamen als körperlose gesellen wieder und wieder,
es war ihnen egal, ob wir sie erleben wollten, sie fragten
uns nicht nach sonnenschein. unsere fabrikneuen
geschmacksknospen verlangten entfaltung, so dass wir
synthetische gummis zwischen die zahnreihen steckten
und auf das künstliche warteten, pinkfarbene pinguine
mit ölpreisbanderolen, gewachste äpfel
oder marshmallowmen. als sie auftauchten,
hielten wir inne und beteten, aber die sprache
nestelte an ihnen herum und nannte sie kreatürlich,
während die abende endlich fremdgingen
in auswärtiger farbe.

septemberkurzschrift

die kürzeldrüse. ihr unverfänglicher
botenstoff, der in die makula drang, die sehgrube
pufferte. die siegel der abbreviaturen – IRQ, IRN, SYR, AFG –
spielten ums schicksal im spiegel von schuldigkeiten.
ich zog die brauen nach. wollte, ich wäre beteiligt gewesen
an jemandes blutdruck. mancher im tross
trug sein erkaltetes kind unter der zunge,
für das er noch immerpfeffermintz lutschte.
der kurze prozess machte klar: es auszustossen
vor heimweh, wär eine fälschung, das sigel des traums
dann sein ende. gebäude links und rechts aller wege
hatten den charme der jahrhunderte längst aufgegeben,
verdrehten die fensteraugen stattdesen. versetzt
in den anklagezustand, witterte ich verzweiflung.
dann wurde mein enkel geboren, der nichts dafür kann,
keine syrische mutter zu haben. dann schlugen sirenen an,
kenterte wieder das boot. dann spielte ich schach
auf dem platz der befreiung, und dann
prozessierte der eine gegen den anderen blick
der schönen europa.

speaking naturally

the nights came time and again like ethereal contracted workmen,
didnt give a damn if we wanted their services, never
inquired regarding our need of sun. our tastebuds,
till then untainted, clamoured for experience
so we sheathed our teeth in synthetic wine gums expecting
something manufactured; pink-hued penguins in branded plastic packs,
apples fabricated in factories, man-shaped
marshmallows. when they showed up we stopped short,
took a moment to utter a prayer, but the words themselves
had a cheeky fumble and pronounced them authentically human
so the nights got on with going astray,
their hues distinctly alien.

september's shorthand

the stenographic gland: its mucus benignly pervading
the retinas central spot, screening the eyes deepest pit;
abbreviatory rubber stamps – IRQ, IRN, SYR, AFG –
a game of mirrors deflecting duty, sealing fates.
i scowled hard, wanting to feel it, share someones heart-ache:
someone in the human convoy, a man
bearing his sons cold corpse under his tongue
like a long-life mint, sucking on and on in longing.
this cursory processing made it clear: to blot it out,
yearn for the return of former times, would be wrong –
would shorten their dream to d then ditch it. facades round about,
both left and right, had long since lost the allures of their bold epoque,
glazed eyes cast instead heavenwards. i imagined me
in the dock, and picked up the scent of sheer desperation.
then my grandson was born, look it wasnt his fault his mum
didnt happen to come from syria. then sirens were blaring,
the boat capsizing again, while i was playing chess in
freedom square, where floats in a procession
displayed competing tableaux of the glorious
goddess europa.

vogelallüren

vögel haben so weltgemacht besserwissende
allüren: tragflächen schultern und los...
sie allein stachen von lesbos aus in die salzluft
der see, den ungeflügelte waren nicht fähig,
die randnotiz zu durchbrechen. schuldig geworden
an meiner gebotenen unschuld, aß ich derweil
und trank, scrabbelte, schlief lang.
lesbos in praller, gefüllter sonne –
ich hatte sie ausgestopft mit waffenständen
und tauchtiefen. als sich das rächte, zog ich am strand
von usedom badeanzüge übereinander. im wasser
schwimmen. nach muscheln tauschen. schöne
beschäftigung, dachte ich, als auch schon wind kam
und mir die haut leckte. getrocknet lag ich später
am strand, die hand überm auge. unverändert
die pralle, gefüllte sonne, lesbos wie usedom drunter,
flügeltiere dazwischen.

birdknacks

birds have got these world-counteracting smart-alec
knacks: techno-turbojet shoulders and hup...
they alone got plucked off lesbos on the salty
sea breeze, while the wingless and flightless were powerless,
even to get a mention in the press. feeling guilty
about my rightful guiltlessness, i ate nonetheless
and drank, played scrabble, slept in.
lesbos under a swollen, bloated sun –
i saw it chocabloc with sentry towers
and darkest depths. defensive, on the beach at usedom
i wore a total riot of bathing attire. swimming
in the sea. diving for mussels. lovely
pastime, i thought, as a breeze lilted over me,
lappping my skin. once dry i lounged later
on the beach, a hand across my eyes. unaltered
the swollen, bloated sun, lesbos just like over on usedom,
hi-tech birdflight between them.

Usedom is a German holiday island destination that was popular
among working people in the former GDR.

Translator's Acknowledgements

Thanks to Jutta Heinen, Christina Les, and Eva Sommer for hours and days spent poring over these poems, and Frieder Sommer for his encyclopaedic back-up support. Thanks to fellow Kathrin Schmidt translator Jamie Osborne; to Sylvie and Jochen in Berlin for weeks of hospitality while I worked in the Amerika Gedenkbibliothek, and to every German-speaking friend I have roped in with my questions, regardless of whether they were into poetry. Thanks to Jean Boase-Beier for all the time she generously gave, emailing her thoughts, ideas and encouragement; also to Jane Draycott, David Morley and the gang of poets at Lumb Bank in 2019 for their *go girl!* morale-boosting. A massive thank you as ever to Naked Eye's Managing Editor Michael Kilyon for his unfailing support, and also, of course, to Alison Marshall, my muse.

My many inspirations include Fiona Sampson who, firstly, taught me poetry translation technicalities in Norwich in 2017 at the BCLT Literary Translation Summer School, an opportunity for emerging translators which I cannot recommend highly enough. Through Fiona I heard of the PoetTrio "collaborative translation" experiment, which I then experienced in action in a workshop with another member of its core team, Francis Jones.

Another big inspiration has been the late Sarah Maguire, proponent of "outsider" translation and founder of London's Poetry Translation Centre where poetry is translated collaboratively in groups (the end product thus being "rooted in modesty"). I have learned tons from taking part in these dynamic, intensely absorbing workshops: all praise to Ed Doegar, Bern Roche Farrelly and Erica Hesketh for their superb facilitation.

Other inspirations include Deborah Smith and Tilted Axis Press with its anti-literary-establishment mission to "shake up contemporary international literature", emphasising the translation from Asian languages of women authors; also Charlotte Ryland who evangelises for translation in schools. Through her workshop programme, children at Short Wood Primary School near Telford translated books from Russian, Polish, Croatian and French – how fantastic is that?

Last but not least I'd like to promote the astonishing website lyrikline.org – a showcase for contemporary European poetry translated into multiple languages.

Biographical Notes

Poet and novelist KATHRIN SCHMIDT was born in 1958 in Gotha in the former German Democratic Republic and lives in Berlin. She trained as a psychologist and later worked as an editor and a social scientist before writing full time. Her voice is held to be distinctly of the east. In 1993 she was awarded the Leonce-und-Lena Preis for her poetry. Multiple awards and residencies for her six poetry volumes and five novels have ensued, a highlight being the German Book Prize for her 2009 novel *Du stirbst nicht* (You're not dying) which beat a shortlist including Nobel Prize winner Herta Muller and was soon translated into thirteen languages. At last an English translation by Christina Les is in progress, to be published 2021, while Schmidt's short story collection *Finito. Schwamm drüber* (It's over. Don't go there) will be published in late 2021 translated by Sue Vickerman. Schmidt's latest poetry collection is *waschplatz der kühlen dinge* (2018), addressing globalisation and migration using the language of politics, advertising and the internet.

SUE VICKERMAN is a writer from the north of England with four works of fiction and five poetry collections to her name. As a result of her country's decision in 2016 to leave the European Union, she forged a translatorial relationship with east-German writer and peer, Kathrin Schmidt, while exploring parallels between Germany's east-west tensions and England's north-south divide, such as the feelings of cultural loss and of being 'left behind' in economic and other respects. In earlier life, Sue Vickerman completed an M.Phil thesis looking at women's spirituality cross-culturally, and much later, an MA in Creative Writing. She has received five writers' awards from the Arts Councils of England and Scotland. She has written for the *Guardian* and *Times Educational Supplement* and her work has appeared in *Poetry Review* and numerous magazines and anthologies. *suevickerman.eu*